*Living
Water*

*To the members and families
of Westminster Presbyterian Church,
Pittsburgh, Pennsylvania,
remembering with joy and thanksgiving
their baptisms*

Living Water

A Guide to Baptism for Presbyterians

JAMES E. DAVISON

Geneva Press
Louisville, Kentucky

Scripture quotations from the New Revised Standard Version of the Bible are copyright © 1989 by the Division of Christian Education of the National Council of the Churches of Christ in the U.S.A. and are used by permission.

Book and cover design by Sharon Adams

First edition
Published by Geneva Press
Louisville, Kentucky

This book is printed on acid-free paper that meets the American National Standards Institute Z39.48 standard. ∞

13 14 15 16 17 18 19 20 21 22 — 10 9 8 7 6

Library of Congress Cataloging-in-Publication Data is on file at the Library of Congress, Washington, D. C.

ISBN-13: 978-0-664-50145-7
ISBN-10: 0-664-50145-1

Contents

INTRODUCTION

As I write these pages, spring has finally arrived. It has been a long winter, but now the rains, coupled with the warmth of the sun's rays, have brought brilliant yellow blossoms to the forsythia. Flowers have begun popping up all over, and the grass is as green as it gets. The effect of rain on the earth strikes me as a vivid reminder of God's promises given in baptism.

The waters of baptism point to the "living water" that Jesus offers in the Gospel of John (4:10). Jesus' words, spoken in the first place to a Samaritan woman who desperately needed a new lease on life, apply to each of us. We all need this renewed, abundant, joy-filled life that comes through God in Christ. The good news of the gospel is that this new life is available to everyone. As the rains fall freely from the heavens, so the life-giving water of Jesus

Christ will be poured down gladly upon all who desire it.

Now, what does this have to do with baptism? The fact that we even ask the question is probably a sign of how completely many Protestant denominations—with Presbyterians at the forefront—have lost sight of the riches of this sacrament in the Christian life. For a variety of reasons, we seem to have little understanding of the meaning and significance of baptism. That is a serious loss because baptism goes back to the earliest days of the church, and it is the foundational sacrament of the faith.

I am convinced that all the key elements of redemption are encompassed in the symbolism of baptism. As we think about this sacrament, or as we watch people receiving baptism during worship, we can recall the essence of what it means to say that "in Christ God was reconciling the world" (2 Cor. 5:19). Consequently, if we really grasp the significance of the sacrament, the very act of remembering our own baptism can become a compelling experience. Martin Luther is a case in point. In times of doubt and worry, he took comfort in the simple thought "I have been baptized!"

Thus, this little book. As you prepare for a baptism in your own family circle or as you explore the meaning of baptism in a study group or as part of your own learning, I hope it will encourage you to reflect on the meaning of this sacrament. If you are studying this book as a part of your family or small group, you may want to read the chapters together. Whether or not you do that, however, be sure to discuss the ideas with others close to you. The questions at the end of each chapter will aid you here.

Use this time before baptism as an occasion for renewed growth and commitment to our Lord. Then come to the baptismal celebration with joy and gladness, giving thanks to God for this life-giving water that is poured on us as a sign of our salvation and our redemption in Jesus Christ.

CHAPTER 1

THE SEAL OF GOD'S GRACE

What is the first thing that comes to mind when you think of baptism? Probably, like many people, your first thought is "water." No wonder! Water is central to baptism. It is so significant, in fact, that we will dedicate the next chapter to some of the main meanings of the water in baptism. However, there is something even more central than water to this sacrament: *grace*. What the water symbolizes (and what the entire baptismal act is intended to demonstrate) is simply this: salvation is a gift of grace. God, out of sheer grace and apart from anything we human beings have to offer, redeems us.

This truth is evident from the very act of baptism. You do not baptize yourself; rather, someone else baptizes you. The first time it is mentioned in the Bible, John the Baptist summons the crowds in preparation for Jesus' coming to receive "a baptism of repentance for the forgiveness of sins" (Mark 1:4–5). We may desire baptism, or we may request it for our child. We certainly have to make our way to the baptismal font. However, from the human standpoint, baptism remains primarily a passive event. Baptism is something you receive, not something you achieve.

Receiving baptism is a supremely telling symbol of God's grace and redemption. Salvation is also something we receive, not something we achieve. Just as God initiated creation in the first place, God also initiates redemption. God's grace comes prior to anything we human beings could hope to accomplish. God gives us salvation; we do not earn or deserve it. That is the heart of the whole gospel, and it summarizes the fundamental insight of the Reformation, when Luther, Calvin, and others reasserted those familiar Pauline words from Ephesians 2:8–9: "For by grace you have been saved through faith, . . . [it is] not the result of works, so that no one may boast."

Therefore, the fact that a person receives baptism, or *is baptized*, makes baptism a particularly good symbol for this intuition about the primacy of God in salvation. Baptism provides a good symbol for other elements of divine salvation as well. Think of the water, the words spoken, the way baptism is done, the location of the font, the presence of the congregation—all can tell us significant things about spiritual realities. I will say more about some of these in the following chapters. Here it is important to consider in a little more depth what we mean when we say that baptism is a "symbol."

Let's step back a moment and start with the word "sacrament." As you probably know, the Roman Catholic tradition holds to seven sacraments: baptism, confirmation, Eucharist, confession, marriage, holy orders (the priesthood), and last rites. Eastern Orthodox communions, it should be noted, do not wish to delimit the sacraments in a specific list. Protestant denominations usually subscribe to only two sacraments: baptism and the Lord's Supper.

There is great divergence among Christian traditions in the way sacraments are understood to operate, but there is nearly universal agreement on the general definition of a sacrament. In the words of St. Augustine, around 400 A.D., a sacrament is "a visible sign of an invisible grace." That is a lovely definition. It is also somewhat vague, which is why most denominations can agree on it! The point is that we are dealing with spiritual realities here; things are happening that we cannot perceive with our physical senses. God's grace is at work inwardly, and by God's grace we are given an outward sign of that activity.

In the Reformed tradition, of which

Presbyterians are a part, we often speak of a sacrament as a "sign and seal" of God's grace, or favor. This is what we mean when we say that the sacraments are "symbols." The sacrament is a sign, in that it sets aside an appropriate element of the physical creation (water; bread and wine) to point towards that unseen reality. The sacrament is also a seal, since it guarantees outwardly and visibly the truth of God's promise of salvation.

You may be aware that some other traditions understand the connection of the "visible sign" to the "invisible grace" in a different way than does the Reformed tradition. For our tradition baptism symbolizes God's working in the person, but the inward, divine action is not necessarily to be identified with the precise moment that the sacrament is administered. Other denominational families (most, in fact) want to make a closer link. They hold that it is at the moment of baptism that God's salvation is given. For them, the sacrament is the divinely appointed means to give grace, and, as a result, baptism is essential for salvation.

Those traditions sometimes think that we Presbyterians undervalue the sacraments, that for us they are really "just" symbols without the riches of God's grace truly attached to them. Presbyterians respond that the alternative is to view baptism as a necessary prerequisite for salvation. Persons who have not been baptized would be, by that very fact, unsaved. To frame the issue in a heartrending fashion: what happens to babies who die before they have been baptized? For the Roman Catholic tradition, this problem has led to the concept of limbo. Unbaptized infants cannot, unfortunately, go to heaven. Nevertheless, God in mercy will not send them to eternal punishment. Rather they will exist in a special borderland called limbo, where they will enjoy a state of blessedness, even though it is not heaven in the full sense.

Other traditions, like the Eastern Orthodox and the Lutheran, which also hold that baptism is the means whereby God dispenses salvation, have been content to say that they simply trust in God's grace to receive into heaven infants who die unbaptized. Gradually, the Catholic Church has been moving toward this same position. As a friend of mine who is a Roman Catholic theologian has put it, for many Catholics, the doctrine of limbo is now in limbo!

To someone from a Baptist or free-church background, all of this may sound unfamiliar. In spite of the kinds of differences I have mentioned above, most of the major traditions within Christianity—Catholic, Eastern Orthodox, Lutheran, Presbyterian, and Methodist—see baptism and the Lord's Supper as sacramental in nature. Historically, however, Baptists and others in the free-church traditions have held to a significantly different view of these two items in the church's life. For them, baptism and the Lord's Supper are not so much "sacraments" as they are "ordinances." In other words, they are things that God commands people in the church to do. They are intended not so much to "show God's grace" but to "show believers' faith."

Remember the question we asked at the beginning of this chapter: What is the first thing that comes to mind when you think of baptism? The answer I suggested was "grace." For the Baptist and free-church traditions, the more appropriate answer would be "faith." In essence, baptism is a sign of belief; it is a pledge that those who are baptized will live a Christian life. To put it another way, if you see baptism as a *sacrament*, the primary actor in baptism is God. If you see it as an *ordinance*, then the primary actor is the human being, and the baptismal act becomes essentially a sign of faith rather than a sign of grace.

Personally, I think that those of us in the sacramental traditions and those in the Baptist and free-church traditions have something to learn from each other. On the one hand, the sacramental traditions have often underplayed the significance of faith in baptism. Baptist and free-church groups remind us of how significant faith is, and I will say more about faith in chapter 4. The sacramental traditions, likewise, have something to offer. Baptism is more than simply a human activity, for there is an essential divine impulse underlying it. The principal meaning of baptism is *God's* signing and sealing of people.

Words and actions work together. There are words involved in the observance of baptism, and the act of baptizing provides a verbal testimony to God's grace within our hearts. At the same time, it moves us more deeply than words alone can do. The words and the action come together, providing a depth and a richness that neither can offer alone. I was reminded of this recently when a good friend's wife died in a tragic accident. In expressing my condolences and sorrow, I gave him a long hug. The hug said more than words could do in that situation— although, of course, saying some words was necessary too. Isn't this an apt illustration of how sacraments operate? Words are pronounced, and an action is performed. The result is a strong testimony to both our minds and our hearts. We hear and see God's grace worked powerfully in our hearts.

All the churches in the sacramental traditions can agree on the general definition of a sacrament, but as we said previously there are major differences of opinion about how sacraments operate. Fortunately, all the groups within this general tradition will accept each other's baptisms. As an example, if you were to come to us from a Roman Catholic background, the Presbyterian Church would not require that you be baptized again. (The same is true in reverse. If a Presbyterian wishes to join a Catholic congregation, his or her baptism would be accepted.)

This mutual acceptance of baptism comes from Ephesians 4:4–5: "There is . . . one baptism." Baptism is the sacrament of initiation into the church, we believe, and so it is not repeatable. As the baptismal service in the Presbyterian *Book of Common Worship* states, "[those baptized] have been received into the one holy catholic and apostolic church." We do not baptize into the *Presbyterian* Church; we baptize into the whole, worldwide family of God. When we are baptized, our baptism, along with the promises of grace it represents, remains with us wherever we go and whatever may happen to us. It is something that we cannot lose, as well as something that cannot be taken away from us.

Once again, I need to mention that the Baptist and free-church traditions take exception to this idea. For them, baptism is only valid if it is performed on persons professing their own faith. Thus it is often called "adult baptism," although the preferred term—since children of various ages are often baptized—is "believer's baptism." In addition, the customary view is that baptism must be by immersion. Consequently, people coming to a Baptist congregation from a sacramental tradition, who in most cases have been baptized as infants (with water sprinkled or poured on their heads), are usually required to be rebaptized.

Notice the word "*re*-baptized." It is the sacramental tradition that sees baptism of an adult already baptized in infancy as a second baptism. From a Baptist perspective, the original "baptism" (of an infant, by sprinkling or pouring) was not a valid baptism in the first place. A person's immersion after confessing his or her own faith is the first baptism. You can see, I'm sure, how troublesome this issue can be. The waters of baptism, which are intended to bring us into one united family of God, have become a source of disunity among God's people. That is tragic.

It will be a long time before we resolve this conflict. A cordial "agreement to disagree" may be the most we can hope for in the near future. As I mentioned previously, the Baptist position puts its finger on some weak spots in the traditional sacramental viewpoint. We have indeed lost something by underplaying the place of faith in the sacrament—and by not getting people very wet when they are baptized! Still, I believe that it is a mistake to make these items absolutely essential to baptism. It sounds perilously close to the kind of legal requirements that Jesus came to free people from in the first place.

That brings us back to the beginning. Baptism points us first and foremost to the grace of God. God has come to us in Jesus Christ with the promise of salvation. Forgiveness, a renewed life in this world, and the promise of eternal bliss are not things that we can achieve or hope to deserve. They come rather from God's gracious hand, stretched out to us in love and compassion. When you think of baptism, think of God and God's grace . . . and be glad!

Some Questions for Thought

Think of some symbols in your life. Why are they important, and what kind of role do they play for you? In what ways do you see symbolism in the baptismal act?

Consider the definition of a sacrament as "a visible sign of an invisible grace." How do you understand it, and how would you apply it to baptism? How do you view the relation of baptism to becoming a Christian?

What does the phrase "one baptism" (Eph. 4:5) mean to you?

Can you explain the distinction between a "sacrament" and an "ordinance"? Which is closest to your own background and viewpoints?

CHAPTER 2

THE WATER OF LIFE

You can get at the meaning of baptism best by focusing on the element used in the sacrament: water. As the title of this chapter suggests, water provides a positive image for baptism. Think of some of the ways in which water can be refreshing. For instance, you might recall taking a long, cool drink after working up a sweat, or bathing in a placid lake on a hot day, or standing in a shower with a stream of water splashing over you in the early morning. All of these seemingly ordinary, everyday activities remind us deep down in our hearts that water is vital to us. More than that: water is absolutely necessary for life.

Just because water is so very beneficial, its life-giving and life-sustaining properties have been recognized from earliest days. Take the ancient Israelites, for example. Living so close to the desert brought relentless reminders of their dependence on rain, on streams, and, indeed, on waters of any kind. Thus, on a regular basis biblical writers mention "pour[ing] water on the thirsty land" (Isa. 44:3); "trees planted by streams of water" (Ps. 1:3); or "burning sand [that] shall become a pool" (Isa. 35:7). Water and life—for Israel, the two can hardly be separated.

Nevertheless, the Israelites could also picture water in a different, much more sinister way. When they looked out on the Mediterranean Sea, they were frightened. The vast expanse of water appeared to be a threat, and the Israelites were afraid to set sail on it. You can almost hear the trembling in people's voices when they speak of it as "the deep," as in this plea in the Psalms: "Do not let . . . the deep swallow me up" (69:15). In this sense, water was not experienced as something life-giving; instead, it was perceived to be a place of danger, destruction, and death.

Water, therefore, can represent life, but it can also represent death. That makes it an especially good symbol for the sacrament that stands at the beginning of the Christian life. Notice what Paul writes: "Do you not know that all of us who have been baptized into Christ Jesus were baptized into his death?" (Rom. 6:3). Paul goes on to portray baptism as a tomb, and that image makes immersion a particularly fitting way to baptize. Entering into deep waters, we are "buried" with Christ, he writes. Thankfully, however, we are covered by the waters only momentarily, and then we emerge again with Christ into new life.

Romans 6 is a crucial biblical passage for understanding baptism. It exhibits both of the meanings that we have been talking about with regard to water. On the negative side, so to speak, there is death—death to the old life. The scriptures are clear from beginning to end about the fact that we human beings are sinful. The word "sin" is not popular in modern culture. As a result, we have developed a host of other ways of describing (or explaining away) the evils, troubles, injustices, and lack of love that abound in our world. Still, whatever we call it, the results are all around us: in society at large, in our neighborhoods, in our schools . . . and in ourselves.

In baptism, God does away with the reign of sin in our lives. Most typically, we say that God "forgives" our sins. The water imagery of baptism, however, enables us to say this in a variety of other ways. For example, God washes sin away, or God buries sin. That is to say, God's destruction of sin's power in our lives is as final as laying someone in a grave. With this in mind, Paul goes on a little later to say that we need to remember that we are "dead to sin" (6:11).

There was a fascinating custom in the early

church that highlights this first side of baptism. Candidates for baptism would first face toward the west. In the symbolism of the setting sun, the ancients saw a picture of the place of darkness and evil. Facing west, persons being baptized would first renounce the devil and his works. Then, turning their backs on the darkness, they would face east to embrace light and the good. The baptismal liturgy still includes vows promising to renounce evil and its power in our lives.

As a footnote to this custom, it is worth noting that churches have often been constructed with this symbolism in mind. In the ancient church, and in many church buildings ever since, the chancel has been placed at the eastern end of the building. Symbolically, therefore, worshipers had their backs to evil and were facing towards the light as they participated in the liturgy. For most of us today, that symbolism is not very strong, partially because electric power has enabled us, in a sense, to turn night into day. Consequently, situating the sanctuary on an east-west axis is usually not one of an architect's chief concerns in planning a new church. (By the way, which direction do you face as you worship in your church?)

Now, getting back to what I am calling the "negative" side of baptism, doing away with sin, a problem may occur to you. How can it be that we are "buried" or "dead to sin" when we know perfectly well that we continue to sin even after baptism? The short answer is that, in baptizing and forgiving us, God breaks the power of sin in our lives. Sin itself does not cease to infect us, but its control over us has been broken. Paul talks about this at length in Romans 6—8. His words are not easy, and they have been subject to many different interpretations. In essence, though, Paul seems to be saying that we now have a new Lord (called at various places "grace," "God," "Christ," "the Spirit") and that we no longer serve an evil master, sin. Still, we have to continually follow this new Lord, for the temptations of sin remain strong around and within us.

There is a "positive" side to the meaning of baptism too. The waters of baptism suggest renewal and rebirth. When we recall that in the beginning waters covered the earth (Gen. 1:1–2), we can say that life in a very real sense emerged from water. When we recall further that all new human life issues from the waters of the womb, then it is an easy step to picturing baptism as a sign—a very compelling sign—of our rebirth in Christ.

What does that life, or rebirth, mean? To Nicodemus, you may remember, Jesus says, "No one can enter the kingdom of God without being born of water and Spirit" (John 3:5). We are talking about a special kind of life here, life on the spiritual plane. It is life given by the Spirit. Put differently, it is life empowered by the Spirit. In Jesus' own baptism by John, the Holy Spirit descends on him like a dove (Mark 1:10). At that point, we might say, the baptism that Jesus offers becomes more than the baptism that Jesus has received. John was a forerunner announcing the fullness of God's coming revelation in Christ, and John's baptism itself offered the first side of that salvation, which is repentance. The second side, however, was reserved for Jesus Christ's coming. Jesus' baptism joined the Spirit to the water. Ever since then, baptism done in Jesus' name not only forgives sin but supplies the Spirit as well. Jesus' own baptism is thus prototypical for all Christian baptisms.

You may be interested to know of a practice in the early church that gets at the heart of this new life in the Spirit in a striking fashion. Immediately following baptism, new believers were sometimes given a new garment to wear. Discarding their old clothing, they would put on clean, white garments to indicate that they were passing into a new state of being, one that involved a morally pure, upright lifestyle. Paul hints at this idea of a change of clothing as marking a change of life already in the New Testament when he writes to the Christians in

Galatia: "As many of you as were baptized into Christ have clothed yourselves with Christ" (Gal. 3:27).

As you can readily imagine, our present-day practice of dressing babies in beautiful white gowns for their baptism goes back to this ancient custom. Notice, though, that the custom is somewhat misleading. The infants arrive dressed in white, which suggests their purity *before* they have gone through the baptismal waters. It is difficult for us to conceive of nearly newborn babies as other than perfect, pure infants. The fact is, however, that all human beings, of whatever age, are in need of the forgiveness and new life that baptism portrays.

Mentioning infants brings to mind a potential difficulty. You may think I am going to raise the issue of infant baptism here. But I am not, at least not directly. I will touch on this thorny topic in chapter 4. What I have in mind is that, for many people, it may seem somewhat disconcerting to speak in strong terms of baptism as dying to the old and being made alive to the new. Does that really go together with those wonderful, almost heavenly babies whom we see brought to the baptismal font? What sense does it make to speak of repentance and forgiveness, sin and judgment, or life and death when we think about them? I suspect that, in infant baptisms, the rich baptismal imagery becomes less vivid, and people tend to view the baptisms as primarily a divine promise of blessing, or preservation from harm.

Granted, the imagery of death and new life may be blunted by the sight of a lovely infant at the font. Nevertheless, the same symbolism and the same meanings apply even to children. The reason is that baptism is a sign for the whole of the Christian life. It guarantees God's commitment to stand by us as long as we live, washing away our sin through Christ's sacrifice and renewing our lives by the power of the Spirit. Whether it is an infant that is baptized, or an elderly adult who has come to faith late in life, the Lord offers this same assurance: one bath, yes, but with cleansing and renewing power that lasts a lifetime.

The water, we have said, provides a compelling symbol for God's work of salvation. How much water is enough? As you know, some groups immerse people, others pour water on their heads, and still others—like many Presbyterians—simply sprinkle water on their foreheads. Given what we have been saying above, it is certainly true that immersing a person completely in a pool of water represents best our dying and rising with Christ. However, the act of pouring is a more appropriate image for the reception of the Holy Spirit. You need only think of the prophecy of Joel quoted by Peter on the day of Pentecost, in which God declares, "I will pour out my Spirit upon all flesh" (Acts 2:17). In terms of symbolism, sprinkling is perhaps the least appropriate method of baptizing, but it is used commonly and will probably continue in practice for a long time to come.

Interestingly, it was not long in the life of the ancient church before this question about how much water should be used arose. An early document called the *Didache*, dating from roughly 100 A.D., advises the following: "If you do not have running water, baptize in some other. If you cannot in cold, then in warm. If you have neither, then pour water on the head three times" (7:2).

Immersion is perhaps the optimal way to baptize, but it is not the only valid way. The prevailing wisdom in Presbyterian circles these days is to continue sprinkling but, at the same time, to use generous amounts of water. It is regularly pointed out that we have become much more restrained in our use of water than were our own American Presbyterian ancestors. In the last century, it was apparently normal to pour water over a person's forehead, letting it fall into a basin. An elder then gave the person a towel to dry themselves.

We would be well advised, I suspect, to return to the custom of making water more visible in the baptismal act. Water is the actual sign and seal of the marvelous things that God has accomplished for us in Jesus Christ, both in forgiving sins and in offering new, abundant life.

Some Questions for Thought

Think of some places in scripture where water plays an important role. (For example, think of the flood in Genesis 6 or the streams of living water in Revelation 22:1–2.) How do these passages help you understand baptism better?

What is the meaning for you of the statement that Jesus Christ gives "living water"?

Which meanings of baptism speak to you most powerfully? How do you apply them to infants?

CHAPTER 3

IN THE NAME OF GOD

Sometimes the question is asked, "What makes a baptism valid?" The usual answer, going all the way back to the early church, is that two things are necessary. First, the baptism must be done using water. Second, it must be performed in the name of the triune God. That's why the baptismal formula in most denominations involves some variation of the words "I baptize you in the name of the Father, the Son, and the Holy Spirit."

There is another common phrase in our baptismal ceremonies: "What is your Christian name?" or "What is the Christian name of your child?" Have you ever thought about the meaning of that question? As you may know, the "Christian" name refers to one's given name. If you are a parent, it is the name you choose for your child. Probably you decide on a particular name for your child for a pragmatic reason. Perhaps the name you choose belongs to someone else in your extended family, or possibly it just has a nice ring to it. You may spend hours and hours considering various names. Expectant parents usually enjoy thinking about names for their unborn child. Some people, though, find the whole process a little unnerving. I know expectant parents who did not finally make up their minds until a nurse asked them their choice of names . . . following the baby's birth!

Perhaps such parents are not so far wrong in hesitating to give a name to their child. After all, this is a weighty decision. The name you choose will go with your child for the whole of his or her life. In a sense, naming your infant is symbolic of your whole relationship to that child. You have given your infant life. It is your care, sustenance, and protection that will enable your child to grow up to become a healthy, strong, upright adult. As that child's parent, you stamp his or her entire life!

I am sure you will not be surprised to hear that the idea of the Christian name originally had great significance. Recall that Jesus renamed Simon, his number-one disciple, "Peter." Recall, too, that the book of Acts tells us about a man named Saul. He was converted on the road to Damascus and came to be known by a new name, "Paul." This set a pattern for the ancient church. As people came to faith in Jesus, especially if they came from Gentile backgrounds, they often took on another name for the precise purpose of marking their new existence as Christians. Their new name indicated that they had received a new life.

When we ask for the Christian name at baptism, not much of that symbolism remains explicit any longer. You may have the feeling that we ministers ask the question simply to be sure that we pronounce the right name. There may be some truth to that, but in fact something much more significant is going on under the surface. By asking for the Christian name, we are consciously de-emphasizing the family name. The purpose here is to say clearly that the person being baptized is becoming part of another family—a much larger family made up of all the people of God. By birth, we are brought into our earthly family; by baptism we are delivered into our divine family. In this new grouping, our primary identity is no longer tied to our earthly family name. Our new family name is much more important. It is the name of God, the triune God.

Notice the words of the baptismal formula: "I baptize you in the name of the Father, and of the Son, and of the Holy Spirit." The phrase "in the name of" is often used in the Bible, and it appears in a variety of ways. To act in the manner or spirit of a person, to speak with that person's authority, to invoke that person's power, to be under his or her protection, or to bear his or her name: these are all examples of how the phrase can be used. With regard to the baptismal formula itself, "being united with Father, Son, and Spirit" or "belonging to the triune God" capture the sense I wish to stress here.

Let's assume, then, that your daughter Teresa or your son Carl is baptized. It is like saying that they become "Teresa, of the triune God" or "Carl, of Christ." Put your own name in one of those phrases. Or put your child's name there. It gives a compelling sense of our membership in the communion of saints when we read our names this personally. It may help to remind us, too, of the fact that by God's grace this family covers a wide area. At Pentecost, Peter summarizes his interpretation of the magnificent events that have been happening with the words "For the promise is for you, for your children, and for all who are far away, everyone whom the Lord our God calls to him" (Acts 2:39).

There should be great comfort in knowing that we, as well as our children, are part of this family that stretches not only across the globe but across the generations as well. Even though we or our children should stray from the faith, we have the assurance that the promise remains valid for us and for them. Like the prodigal son, whom the father welcomes home, our place in the family is permanently secure. Following a baptism in the Irish Presbyterian Church, the minister says to the family, "Your child is now a member of the church universal. There will always be a place for your child in it."

Doesn't all of this mean that there is a sense in which your day of baptism is equally as significant as the day of your birth? Couldn't "baptism day" be a day for remembrance and celebration just like a birthday is? Some time ago, a personal experience brought this home to me powerfully. I came across my mother's baptismal certificate. Born and baptized early in the twentieth century, she received a lovely certificate of baptism. It is nine-by-sixteen inches, inscribed with graceful lettering, printed with a five-color design, and held in a decorative frame. The black-ink, five-by-seven-inch certificates we give out following baptisms look dull and commonplace by comparison.

Most of us will probably not begin framing baptismal certificates and mounting them on the walls of our homes, but it would certainly be useful to begin making more of the anniversaries of baptisms in our families. For instance, on each person's baptism day there could be a small celebration. It need not be elaborate—just festive enough to make it clear that this is a special day for a special person whom God loves.

Parents could tell children who have been baptized as infants what that day was like. Those baptized at an older age could recall what they felt and experienced at their baptisms. The family could read together a few brief biblical passages about the meaning of baptism, such as those listed at the end of this booklet. A celebration like this may become a wonderful time for family members to share their faith with each other as they talk about the meaning of this sacrament.

Since baptism draws us into a wider family, baptism days could be observed in church as well as in homes. Church schools could celebrate the day of baptism for the children in their classes. Many classes already celebrate children's birthdays, but so do most elementary school classes. In church school, why not substitute baptism day for birthday celebrations? One caution is necessary, however. For various reasons some children may not (yet) have been baptized. A teacher will need to handle such situations carefully so that these children do not feel excluded.

The communal nature of baptism has serious implications for how we celebrate the sacrament. It is certainly true that baptism is a family affair, and it is not surprising that extended families often gather for a kind of reunion when a baptism is scheduled to be celebrated. Nevertheless, if you think about what I said above, you will realize that it is not really sufficient to have only the family—however large it may be—attend a baptism. A number of denominations do celebrate baptisms as special ceremonies in the presence only of family members and close friends. In the Presbyterian tradition, however, we call such an event "private baptism," and we believe that it is not really a wise practice. It obscures the important dimension of the presence of the whole family of God in baptism.

We believe that baptism is best conducted in a service of worship where a congregation has come together to praise God. Having a regular congregation in attendance is crucial, because the assembled congregation functions as the local representative of the whole family of God. As such, the congregation welcomes those who are baptized into the church universal (the "catholic" church spoken of in the Apostles' Creed), and it promises to help these newly baptized persons to grow and mature in their faith.

One effective way to make this aspect of baptism clear, by the way, is to perform baptism in the center of the congregation itself. You may have seen this done in a church with a movable baptismal font, but it is also possible to achieve the same result by placing a large basin in the center of the congregation for the baptismal ceremony. As the minister and family, along with the person being baptized, stand in the midst of the people, the linkage between congregation and baptism becomes crystal clear. By the waters of baptism this person is being joined to God's people, and the congregation in turn promises its nurture, support, and fellowship.

This is a good place to say more about the placement of fonts in church buildings. As I mentioned earlier, the location of the font is one of the many significant symbolic elements in the baptismal ceremony. In the early church, fonts were often placed at the doorway of the building. This location served to indicate that people enter the church through baptism. The Catholic tradition continues this practice today. The custom of dipping your fingers in a basin of holy water situated near the entrance, which you see regularly in Catholic churches, is meant to remind people coming to worship of their own baptism.

Protestant churches have tended to place the font at the front of the sanctuary. From a practical point of view, this makes it easier for people to see baptisms being performed. At a deeper level, the intention is to illustrate the connection of this sacrament to both the preaching of the Word and the Lord's Supper. Preaching and sacraments are two forms in which God's Word comes to us. We call them the "spoken" Word of God and the "visible" Word of God. Seeing the water of baptism and the elements of communion helps to seal in a perceptible way God's gracious promises that we have heard read in the scriptures and preached from the pulpit.

Where the font is placed—whether at the doorway, or near the pulpit and table, or in the center of the congregation—does say subtle but highly important things regarding baptism. Unfortunately, in the Presbyterian tradition there has been a tendency to treat the baptismal font as something less important than the pulpit and the table. Presbyterian baptismal fonts have often been rather small, and sometimes even placed "out of the way." I have heard of an instance in one church where the font was actually kept in a closet, to be brought out only when needed. Recently, there has been greater recognition of the value in emphasizing the font more effectively. Fonts are being made larger, and they are also being placed in more conspicuous positions. The overall effect, naturally, is to foster an increased awareness of the import of baptism for the whole of our Christian life and experience.

Some Questions for Thought

> How do you feel about your name, and what does it mean? Does it have any special Christian significance?

> Think of the Christian names of your children or others in your family.

Why were those names chosen? Have they continued to hold any special significance as time has passed?

Find out the baptismal days of your family members. Share any memories that people, such as parents and grandparents, may have about what occurred on those days. Do you have any pictures or certificates from those occasions?

What does it mean to you to say that baptism joins you, or your children, to a new, universal family?

Where have you seen baptismal fonts located in churches, and where have you yourself seen baptisms take place? Do any of those locations speak to you in a special way?

CHAPTER 4

A STATEMENT OF FAITH

In the first chapter, I highlighted the fact that the initiative in baptism comes from God. God is the "primary actor," you might say, and the sacrament symbolizes the priority of divine grace in our lives. That human beings are essentially passive during the act of baptizing is a fitting reminder of this fundamental truth. Now it is time to focus our attention on the other side of baptism.

God is the primary actor in baptism, yes, but God is not the *only* actor. The person being baptized is a kind of "secondary actor," with his or her own role to play. To use the word "secondary" with regard to those who are baptized, therefore, does not mean that they are passive or lifeless. Rather, at baptism people are "receptive." Baptism symbolizes God's gracious gift of forgiveness and new life. It also symbolizes a human being's reception of that gift in gratitude and faith.

As we think about this second side of baptism, we need to remember that the most original form of baptism involves converts to Christianity. Most of us are accustomed to seeing the baptism of infants, and it may seem strange to speak of faith in connection with the person being baptized. In fact, however, the baptism of infants is a derivative form of the sacrament. We will talk more about it later in this chapter after we talk about baptism in its original form.

The essence of the human side in baptism is that a person affirms his or her faith. It is an affirmation of a particular faith, to a particular group of people. Let's start with the group first. We sometimes speak of baptism as being a public profession of faith. Often, it is assumed that "public" refers to someone standing before the world at large to make this profound profession of faith in Christ. That may sometimes be the case, but more often than not the sacrament occurs within the midst of a believing congregation.

In times of persecution, when becoming a convert to Christianity may make one liable to discrimination or even death, baptisms are usually conducted in secret, out of sight of the eyes of the state. The important thing is that, on the human side, the act of baptism is an affirmation to the church that a person wishes to join the Christian congregation in worshiping and serving God.

This affirmation is made to a particular group of people. It also confirms that the person believes what the church believes. It is a profession of a particular faith. What is that faith? Plainly, it is the faith that is expressed in the baptismal formula; it is faith in the God who is "Father, Son, and Holy Spirit."

You may be aware that the familiar confession of faith that we call the Apostles' Creed originated in the context of baptism. Very early in the life of the church, it became customary to ask questions of those who wished to be baptized. As you can imagine, the questions centered on the core beliefs of the church, and therefore, on the Trinity. An early version of the questions has been preserved for us by Hippolytus, who lived in Rome around 215 A.D.:

> Do you believe in God the Father Almighty?
>
> Do you believe in Christ Jesus, the Son of God, who was begotten by the Holy Spirit from the Virgin Mary, who was crucified under Pontius Pilate, and died (and was buried) and rose the third day living from the dead, and ascended into the heavens, and

> sat down on the right hand of the
> Father, and will come to judge the
> living and the dead?
>
> Do you believe in the Holy Spirit, in the
> holy church, and in the resurrection
> of the body?

As time passed, the answers to the baptismal questions continued to become more and more detailed. Somewhere along the line, the responses were joined together into the familiar three-point affirmation of faith that we call the Apostles' Creed:

The Apostles' Creed

I believe in God the Father Almighty,
Maker of heaven and earth,

And in Jesus Christ his only Son our Lord;
who was conceived by the Holy Ghost,
born of the Virgin Mary, suffered under
Pontius Pilate, was crucified, dead, and
buried; he descended into hell; the third
day he rose again from the dead; he
ascended into heaven, and sitteth on the
right hand of God the Father Almighty;
from thence he shall come to judge the
quick and the dead.

I believe in the Holy Ghost; the holy
catholic Church; the communion of saints;

the forgiveness of sins; the resurrection of the body; and the life everlasting. Amen.

Don't let the name, the Apostles' Creed, mislead you. The text of the creed as we have it does not date from the time of the apostles themselves. It is rather rooted in their teachings, and the church intended it to be a faithful rendering of what they believed. As Hippolytus shows, much of its content was already in use very early, but the text continued to be refined, and various versions circulated in different parts of the Roman world for centuries.

There is a further point worth noting about this baptismal creed: it is a product of what we call the Western church. It developed in the western half of the Roman Empire. Its use has been limited to traditions that have grown up in that area. That includes, specifically, the churches in the Roman Catholic and Protestant traditions. Eastern Orthodox communions have never adopted it. Instead, they have embraced the more elaborate Nicene Creed, which has been the center of their faith and worship ever since it was approved and revised at councils of the whole church in the fourth century:

The Nicene Creed

We believe in one God,
the Father, the Almighty,

maker of heaven and earth,
of all that is, seen and unseen.

We believe in one Lord, Jesus Christ,
the only Son of God,
eternally begotten of the Father,
God from God, Light from Light,
true God from true God,
begotten, not made,
of one Being with the Father;
through him all things were made.
For us and for our salvation
he came down from heaven,
was incarnate of the Holy Spirit and the
  Virgin Mary
and became truly human.
For our sake he was crucified under Pontius
  Pilate;
he suffered death and was buried.
On the third day he rose again
in accordance with the Scriptures;
he ascended into heaven
and is seated at the right hand of the Father.
He will come again in glory to judge the
  living and the dead,
and his kingdom will have no end.

We believe in the Holy Spirit, the Lord, the
  giver of life,
who proceeds from the Father and the Son,
who with the Father and the Son is
  worshiped and glorified,
who has spoken through the prophets.

We believe in one holy catholic and
    apostolic church.
We acknowledge one baptism for the
    forgiveness of sins.
We look for the resurrection of the dead,
    and the life of the world to come. Amen.

The Western churches, too, accept the
Nicene Creed, but for a variety of historical and
cultural reasons, the Apostles' Creed took firm
hold in the West and has continued to be used
more frequently than the Nicene Creed.

Nevertheless, both East and West agree on
the value of creeds in the context of baptism.
Eastern Orthodox communions have always
used the Nicene Creed extensively in their baptismal liturgy. Often, Western churches will
recite the Apostles' Creed at baptisms. The
Presbyterian *Book of Common Worship* also
encourages use of the Apostles' Creed during
celebrations of baptism. In my experience, however, Presbyterian churches sometimes do not
do this, either because the creed is recited each
week elsewhere in the worship service, or
because—more pragmatically, but perhaps less
justifiably—concern for the length of the service leads ministers to omit it.

The regular use of a creed at baptism is a force-
ful reminder that an essential element of the
sacrament is a profession of faith by the whole
church, including the person who is being

baptized. In the act of receiving God's grace in Christ through the waters of baptism, the person affirms before the assembled congregation that he or she shares the same faith and wishes to serve the same Lord. Recitation of either the Apostles' or the Nicene Creed is a wonderful sign that this newly baptized person is joining "with all the saints" who, from generation to generation, have confessed the same creed in many places and in many centuries.

The act of baptism is also an affirmation of faith, a promise to live according to the way of Jesus Christ. In the Great Commission, recorded in Matthew 28:20, Jesus commands his followers to go into the world to make disciples. How? By baptizing, says Jesus, and by "teaching them to obey everything that I have commanded you." A vow of obedience to the words of Jesus is implicit in receiving the baptismal waters. Earlier, I referred to Galatians, where Paul reminds his readers that "as many of you as were baptized into Christ have clothed yourselves with Christ" (3:27). For Paul, this presupposes that believers in Christ will strive, with the help of God's Spirit, to be led by that Spirit (5:16), avoiding destructive desires and practices and following a style of life that is in accord with Jesus Christ (5:14–26). I will say more about this in the next chapter.

I have been underscoring the fact that there are two sides to baptism. If we draw both sides together now, they provide a compelling summary of the gospel. First and foremost is God, who in the water of baptism promises us forgiveness of our sins and a new, fresh life, undergirded by the Spirit in the community of the church. In response, we receive this water, affirming in turn our trust in this gracious, triune God, our promise to live a Christian life of love, and our desire to be joined to the community of faith.

If the original form of baptism involves both the divine and the human sides—God's gracious gift and a person's response of faith—what are we to make of the baptism of infants? How can little babies exercise faith? How can they hear and grasp God's word of forgiveness and the promise of new life? If they cannot, what is our justification for baptizing them? This issue has caused serious disputes and division ever since the time of the Reformation. Those of the Baptist and free-church traditions, who place renewed emphasis on this second side of baptism, have concluded that only those who can consciously confess their faith ought to receive baptism. In light of the comment in Ephesians 4:5 that there is "one baptism," it is ironic that the controversies over infant baptism have been so heated that we might almost call baptism "the waters that divide."

Martin Luther once tried to solve the problem by suggesting that infants themselves may possibly exercise a kind of "infant faith," but most denominations that baptize babies have not followed this path. Most traditions say that, when infants are baptized, faith is offered on their behalf by other people—either parents, sponsors ("godparents"), or the congregation as a whole. The underlying assumption is that, because children are part of a given family, they participate in the faith of that family as well; as a result, they should not be excluded from the blessings and promises of faith simply because they are too young to understand and accept this faith in a conscious way.

Often, those who practice infant baptism will cite the Old Testament custom of circumcising infant boys on the eighth day, pointing out that the Israelites always viewed children as integral participants in the covenantal people, belonging as fully to Israel as any adult. Just as the Israelites recognized an age of accountability, denoted by the bar mitzvah ceremony, so churches that practice infant baptism establish a time for children to affirm their own faith. Usually, this is connected to a course of study, such as a catechism class. Different names are used—for example, confirmation class, communicants' class, or commissioning class—but the essence is the same. It is a time of preparation so that children can profess for themselves the faith affirmed on their behalf at their baptism.

Most Christian communions accept and practice infant baptism. The Baptist tradition, however, which is particularly strong in North America, has continued to insist that faith be exercised by the individual being baptized—at the time of baptism. Here I do not want to go into the details of the arguments advanced by each side. Let me just say that both sides can point to strong scriptural evidence for their respective positions. That is precisely the problem! Neither case can be proved conclusively.

It is not likely that the disagreements on this issue will be resolved soon. The recommendation included in a 1982 ecumenical study document, *Baptism, Eucharist and Ministry*, seems to me to be the wisest and most promising approach at present. The document advises that communions on both sides of the infant baptism debate agree to recognize each other's practices in good faith as "equivalent alternatives."

Within our own Presbyterian Church (U.S.A.), the *Book of Order* advises acceptance of both alternatives while strongly encouraging baptism of infants. "Without undue haste, but without undue delay" are the operative words (W-2.3012). Our denomination stresses that a child's baptism before he or she is conscious of what is happening is an especially good reminder of the way God's grace comes to all of us in the first place. At whatever age we are, God calls us and works in our lives and hearts before we are aware of it. In other words, before we love God, God loves us.

One final point before ending this chapter: if infant baptism is to mean anything, then the parents (one of them, at least) need to be actively involved in training the child in the faith so that their child does in fact eventually affirm his or her own faith. Some parents who otherwise are not involved in a congregation—and they can be found in all traditions—feel it is important to have their child "done." They bring the child for a festive celebration of baptism, but they apparently have no sense of the fact that the sacrament involves promises by them and the congregation for the ongoing Christian nurture of their child.

Personally, I find this attitude hard to understand. An infant's baptism without the presence of a believing, active parent empties the vows taken by both the parents and the congregation of their meaning. The role of the congregation is undermined because the members cannot fulfill their vows. It is likely that none of the riches that baptism stands for will be made known in a convincing way to the child. It is much more meaningful when parents present their child at the font with the awareness that they will need God's help, as well as the support of the congregation, to fulfill their responsibilities in guiding this new, precious life into a living relationship with the living Lord.

Some Questions for Thought

Think back to the time when you were first conscious of your own faith in Christ. What were the circumstances? How has that influenced your life since then?

If you were designing the service of baptism, would you be inclined to include a creed? Why or why not? If you would, what would recitation of a creed mean to you?

The "second side" of baptism, the human response, indicates a promise both to trust in Christ and to live in accord with his teachings. Practically speaking, how do you put that into effect for yourself or your child? What sorts of things do you think you can plan to do to assure that the vows you take will be meaningful?

CHAPTER 5

THE MINISTRY
OF THE BAPTIZED

Baptism is the sacrament of incorporation into the Christian faith. It is a beginning point, not the final destination. As important as it is, baptism is simply the first, decisive step in what is intended to be a lifelong, vital relationship with Jesus Christ. Similarly we say, "A wedding is not a marriage." A wedding joins a man and woman together in marriage, but the test of the faithfulness, the goodness, and the value of a marriage will come only through the days, years, and even decades in which the couple strives to live together, forgiving and loving each other.

The same is true of baptism. The Swiss Reformer Ulrich Zwingli once likened baptism to a monk's robe. When the novice puts on the robe, he is indeed fully a monk. Still, there is a great difference between him, as he begins his journey in the monastic order, and an aging monk who has worn the robe for years and years. The latter knows the meaning of being a monk through a lifetime of experiencing its trials and tribulations, as well as its joys and blessings. Baptism, too, is a starting point. The question that this fact raises is, Where do we go from here?

In the first place, the answer is simply this: relying on God's promised forgiveness and grace, we are to live out the vows we have made at baptism. I mentioned this briefly already in the last chapter, when I referred to Paul's admonition that we are to "clothe ourselves with Christ" (Gal. 3:27). A certain style of life is intended to follow after our baptism, one that honors Christ and embraces his commandments as our pattern of living. Paul often speaks of this in terms of the Spirit. We are to "walk by," or "be led by," or "bear the fruit of" the Spirit.

You find the same thing at the beginning of the third Gospel when John the Baptist inaugurates his message of repentance and baptism. Luke tells us that the crowds were asking him, "What then should we do?" (3:10). Tax collectors and soldiers asked similar questions, leading John to provide specific instructions regarding how they should live from that point onwards (3:11–14). From beginning to end in the New Testament, ethical implications are inherent in receiving baptism. You might even say that the New Testament was written for two purposes: first, to draw us to the waters of baptism; and second, to encourage and guide us in leading a life appropriate to people who have been baptized.

We are thus summoned to fulfill the God-given call we received at baptism, as is implied in the title of this chapter: "The *Ministry* of the Baptized." Recent studies of ordination and ministry have begun to rediscover something that has been undervalued for much of the history of the church. Baptism itself should be understood as an ordination to ministry in the church. Each of us who is baptized receives the laying on of hands and is thereby commissioned to perform service within the congregation.

This is quite a change in viewpoint. Ever since the early history of the church, we have tended to see ordination as something that applies only to special offices in the church. Unfortunately, concentration on the clergy and other specialized ministries has had the detrimental effect of encouraging the assumption that only those who have been ordained to office have vital ministries to perform. Laypeople may do any number of things to help out in the church, but what they are doing does not really qualify as "ministry."

The Reformers of the sixteenth century recognized the problems here, but the churches of the Reformation have not by any means escaped them. In the Presbyterian Church, we recognize three offices: ministers, elders, and deacons. Even though we say everyone is called to serve in the church, we speak of people elected to these three offices as ordained to special ministries in the life of the church. The distinct impression this leaves, unfortunately, is that those who are not ordained to such offices do not have a ministry to perform.

Across the board, thankfully, we are coming to recognize that all Christians are ministers, set apart by baptism to serve Christ in a whole host of ways. Baptism is the first and primary ordination that any Christian can receive. The ministries we engage in will differ, of course, because God has created great variety and diversity in the human community. Yet without doubt we are each given significant ministries, and we are called in our baptisms to take up those ministries joyfully and confidently, trusting in the Spirit to direct, guide, and empower us.

It is important to say a word here about a popular teaching in evangelical and charismatic circles these days. It is the concept of "the baptism in the Holy Spirit." The phrase is used to speak of a powerful experience in the Christian life that lifts one beyond a humdrum faith to a vital, robust existence in the power of the Holy Spirit. When you have received this experience, often but not always accompanied by speaking in tongues, you will find yourself living a victorious Christian life and exercising gifts given by the Spirit.

As I said, this is a popular viewpoint. Recently, I spent some time looking for books on baptism in a Christian bookstore. When I was unable to locate any, I asked a clerk if the store stocked books on the subject. The clerk gave me a quizzical look and finally said, "Baptism . . . Do you mean *water* baptism?" The store did not stock any titles on baptism, but there were a number of books on "baptism in the Spirit." This experience brought home to me how completely water and Spirit have become separated for many Christian people in our day. No longer do they understand baptism as the sign of God's forgiving of sin and giving of new life in the Spirit. Water and Spirit have undergone a "divorce," and these people clearly take "water baptism" to be of much less import than "Spirit baptism" for the Christian life.

Let me say that there is seeming support for a doctrine of the "baptism in the Holy Spirit" in certain passages in the book of Acts. A closer reading of these sections, however, along with a careful study of Paul's theology of faith, baptism, and Spirit, makes it clear that this separation of two kinds of baptism involves a profound misunderstanding of the biblical material. The worst result is that it drives a wedge between Jesus Christ and the Spirit. It implies that there are two levels to Christian faith: a basic level when you receive Christ, and a second, richer one when you receive the power of the Spirit. With this approach, it is hard to avoid the temptation to see the first stage as made up of non-committed people ("carnal" Christians is a phrase sometimes used), while reserving the second stage for those who are truly committed and Spirit-led.

We need to recognize that baptism, as a sign and seal of new life in Christ, signifies this new life fully and completely. As we mentioned in chapter 2, it includes the Holy Spirit. Therefore, it includes the gifts of that Spirit as well. In the ancient church, and in the Orthodox and Catholic traditions today, this has been accentuated by including a rite of anointing with oil along with baptism. The practice goes back to the Old Testament, where anointing carried the connotation of empowering a person with God's Spirit for service. You may remember that the term used of Jesus, "Messiah," itself means "the anointed One." It should not be surprising, therefore, to read that at his baptism Jesus received the Holy Spirit.

The renewing waters of baptism carry with them the promise that God will empower us with the Spirit and give us gifts to serve in the

church. Each person has talents that can con-
tribute to the well-being of the whole congregation. If you read the various lists in the Pauline
epistles (Rom. 12:6–8; 1 Cor. 12:8–10, 28; Eph.
4:11–12), you will be surprised at how many
widely divergent activities are perceived to be
"gifts." Some sound extraordinary and marvelous, but most seem mundane and normal.
The fact that the different lists mention so
many, with no apparent order or structure, suggests that the early Christians did not have a def-
inite list of talents. Instead, any activity that
served the church in a meaningful way was
regarded as a gift. Whatever that activity might
be, the same instruction applied: "Like good
stewards of the manifold grace of God, serve
one another with whatever gift each of you has
received" (1 Peter 4:10).

Baptism is at one and the same time a
promise and a call. It is a promise that each of
us has been given gifts by the Spirit, and it is
a call to employ those gifts for the benefit of
the whole church. The issue, then, is to put the
promise and call of baptism into practice in our
daily lives. As you prepare for a celebration of
baptism, reflect on the consequences of this
sacrament for your own life—whether you
yourself are being baptized or whether someone else in your family is receiving the
sacrament.

If you are studying the sacrament of baptism, reflect on the meanings of baptism and how these promises and words of grace are experienced throughout the Christian life. If you are yourself soon to be baptized, reflect how these promises and words of grace are for you. If you are a parent bringing a child for baptism, I encourage you to remember that all of the aspects of baptism mentioned in this book apply to your child. Bear in mind that the effects promised in the baptismal waters are likely to take place only if you consciously and consistently nurture your child's growth in faith. Talk with your child about your own faith. Teach your child to pray. Bring him or her to church to worship and learn. Help your child to grow up knowing that he or she not only has a place in the congregation but also has gifts to offer in service and ministry.

Along the way, don't forget that your child's primary teacher will be you! It is your own life and actions that will be most influential. I also encourage you to find things that you can do together as families in your congregation. To a high degree, it is the importance you attach to your own family's participation in the family of faith that will determine how well your child grows and develops in faith.

Martin Luther once said that baptism is a

sacrament for the whole of life. It stands at the beginning of our Christian experience, but it is like a beacon illuminating the whole of our walk with God in this world. It points to God's gracious forgiveness of our sins and failures; it promises us continuing new life by the power of the Spirit in the family of the church; and it calls us to constancy in professing our faith and in fulfilling our Spirit-given ministries for the good of the whole body of believers.

As you experience baptism yourself or in your family, I hope that you will take the opportunity to reflect on all the things that the water of baptism signifies. You may wish to renew your own baptismal vows in some way at this time. In any case, rejoice in your baptism, and let it encourage you as it did Luther, who found reassurance, confidence, and security in the simple thought "I have been baptized!"

Some Questions for Thought

What difference does it make to you to think of baptism as "ordaining people to ministry"?

Look at the lists of gifts, or talents, in the Pauline letters. What are your impressions? Take some time thinking about what your own, and your family members', gifts may be.

How do you help each other in your family to grow in faith? Can these discussions of baptism be of any assistance in that regard?

What do you think of the idea of looking at baptism as an "ordination"?

CPSIA information can be obtained
at www.ICGtesting.com
Printed in the USA
BVHW03s1624200418
513905BV00008B/71/P